Woodshedding: What No One Tells You About Practice

A Musician's Guide

Charlie Tottman

Published in 2022

Edited by Richard Sheehan
www.richardmsheehan.co.uk

Front Cover Design by 100Covers.com

ISBN: 978-1-7397298-0-6

ABOUT THE AUTHOR

Charlie Tottman

Charlie grew up in Woking and started to play the guitar at age 15. He developed an early obsession with practice and began teaching guitar in 2006. He has since taught hundreds of students all over the world how to play.

Charlie is the author of two instructional ebooks, has delivered seminars and worked as an examiner for The London College of Music, and has performed gigs throughout the UK & Europe.

Charlie lives in Guildford with his wife Jessica, daughter Clara and their cat, Warren Buffett.

For my wife Jessica.

Guildford, England

2022

INTRODUCTION

During the last twelve or so years that I've taught guitar, the one thing that has had the biggest impact on the progress of my students at all levels is their understanding of *how* to practise.

Most people assume that *practising* and *playing* an instrument are the same thing. The truth is that while playing an instrument is enjoyable, practising can sometimes feel a little repetitive. One of my students recently remarked on their experience of practice: 'If it's not boring, then you're not doing it right.'

I've written this book because I want to change the way that people think about practising music. One of the key aspects of the guidance that I provide for my own students is helping them to discover how they can use their own practice time effectively. While students are often bombarded with various learning materials and given plenty of stuff to learn, they are generally not provided with enough direction in relation to how they should be digesting all of this material or shown what 'good' practice should actually look like.

I want people to become aware of the common

factors influencing their ability to progress, helping them to realise that these same factors are probably affecting everybody else. The first part of this book will deal with the barriers that musicians face when practising an instrument, identifying why most people find it so difficult to get better at music and why I'm not a big fan of the word 'talent'. I'll then go on to talk about a concept referred to as 'effective practice'. I'll discuss what it is, why it works and explain how anyone is able to implement it. Finally, I'll delve deeper into the thought processes that surround the entire process and demonstrate how an understanding of what influences your own willingness and attitudes to practice can change everything. I've also included a handy practice plan which will help you to apply the ideas and approaches discussed in this book, encouraging you to be creative with your musical goals.

What do you want?

It's my belief that before deciding to study music, whether that be as a full-time pursuit or hobby, you should always ask yourself the blindingly simple question: 'What do you want?'

So many people throw themselves into projects, meetings, exercise regimes and negotiations without really giving a serious thought to what it is that they actually want. In this instance, we could maybe tweak the question slightly to: 'What is it that you want to achieve?' It's no surprise that many people neglect to think about this, even when they start to become serious about playing an instrument. While I agree that it all sounds a bit dramatic and seemingly out of place in a discussion regarding music practice, how can you expect to get started without a rough plan of what you'd like to achieve?

If you've adopted a casual approach to learning music, it's easy to assume that you needn't think about anything as dramatic sounding as 'goal setting' but even music hobbyists should aim to establish even just a rough set of objectives. It's also important to think about how you might manage your own expectations. Incidentally, addressing one's expectations is one of the first things that I believe a good tutor should run through with their students.

Who is this book for?

My perspective as a guitar player and tutor inform how I think about practising, but the principles outlined within this book can certainly be applied to other instruments. Regardless of your level or playing experience, I want this book to encourage you to think about how you approach practice, whether you do it for ten minutes or ten hours a day.

While a lot of the language in the book is more specific to the guitar, there are plenty of ideas here for all musicians. Whether you play professionally or you're a complete beginner, my hope is that the concepts and approaches discussed will encourage you to think differently and change the way that you practise.

My own struggles with practice and progress

Throughout the eighteen years or so that I have been playing the guitar, there have been periods of time where I have spent a lot of time practising, remaining consistent and making good progress. However, I've also wasted a lot of time because I didn't know how to organise myself and prioritise what I wanted to achieve.

Because there were aspects of learning music that I've always struggled with, I'd assumed that I lacked any real, natural musical talent. This would, in turn, persuade me that practising wouldn't really help, which then inevitably became a self-fulfilling prophecy – this held me back, impacting my confidence and ability. I've since come to better understand the learning process, while appreciating what a negative impact the notion of preconceived natural ability can actually have. I've had no shortage of bad auditions, gigs and musical experiences that didn't go my way, but I want to assure people that negative experiences are an essential part of the learning process. Failure at any level provides you with the valuable feedback you'll rely on to improve your ability and build your own personal resilience.

So, let's get started by pulling apart the process. First we look at some of the problems that we all encounter as musicians.

PART 1: PROBLEMS

Author Stephen Covey, in his book *The 7 Habits of Highly Effective People,* describes how the majority of people don't know how to practise a skill: 'From golf to playing the violin, having twenty years of practice will often mean that they've had twenty years of repeating the same mistakes. Some people say they have twenty years, when in reality, they only have one year's experience, repeated twenty times.'

The problem with 'talent'

'Talent' is a word which is grossly overused in my opinion, and to make matters worse, people are keen to construct their own interpretation of its definition. Some people perceive it to be an indication of natural ability, perhaps leading people to believe that they are 'gifted' or in some way entitled to achieve, regardless of effort. Others assume that someone who is 'talented' is just really very, very good at something and has clearly put a lot of work in.

My view is that real danger arises from students being told that they possess 'natural' talent or that they are in some way gifted. In the case of students who do display some form of natural ability, this can provide them with a sense of entitlement and perhaps even a subconscious feeling that actually they don't need to work that hard to achieve. This may be okay as they progress through their formative years, but as they start to become more deeply involved in the music learning process, they inevitably start to realise that supposed 'talent' will only get you so far.

For a student who then starts to become serious about music, perhaps even considering it as a career, they can run into real problems. How can a student be expected to 'work' or 'practise' if they've had no prior experience of doing so? If they've always just been able to 'do it' in a musical sense, how are they going to summon the desire to suddenly start putting the work in?

In my opinion, telling young students that they are naturally 'gifted' or that they were born talented is short-sighted, careless and unfair. The word 'talent' will have undoubtedly been responsible for some students not fulfilling anything even close to their potential. Conversely, those who feel the need to work hard and diligently to achieve their goals will always understand the level of practice required in order to achieve results. Whether they are conscious of it or not, they know how to practise because they *had* to.

The problem with being 'talented'

Once someone has been labelled as 'talented', it can also negatively influence their attitude towards taking risks. They may be less motivated to perform, attend auditions or write music because they dread the consequences of failure. However, failing repeatedly is an essential part of effective practice, and without opening yourself up to failure, you're going to find it impossible to improve your musical ability.

The nurture vs nature debate is an absolutely fascinating subject, and if you feel a need to delve more deeply into it, I would highly recommend reading both Matthew Syed's *Bounce* and *The Talent Code* by Daniel Coyle, both of which uncover some fairly compelling examples, contradicting the notion that high achievers are supposedly born with natural ability.

How does this relate to your own practice? Wherever you stand on the nature vs nurture debate, I would encourage you to consider that you are more likely to achieve your goals if you're able to dispel any preconceptions (positive or negative) that you may have regarding your own ability. I think it's important to be aware of your own perceptions; have you ever been told that you were 'talented'? Without being aware of it, this may be influencing your own attitude towards working on your music. Conversely, if you feel that you've always struggled, and concluded that you have never had any musical ability whatsoever, then I can assure you that you're allowing yourself to succumb to defeat too easily.

If you want to do it, you can do it. You just need to work and practise a little smarter.

The problem with other people

Along with the many advantages that technology brings for those of us making or learning music, there are plenty of negative aspects too.

It's impossible to not compare yourself with others, especially in the modern age where we find ourselves increasingly ever more connected, engaged and fascinated with the lives of everyone else. For some people, it seems, the pursuit of music has almost started to develop some sort of competitive edge, whether it's the posting of videos or sharing of achievements. To survive in the modern age, you have to see past the noise and constantly remind yourself of why you actually started learning music in the first place.

It's easy to watch others performing and occasionally feel envious of their skills, but remember that there are probably a number of people who may watch or listen to *you* play and possess an equally similar degree of envy or awe. The feeling of wishing that you were as 'good' as someone else will not make you any happier and probably won't improve your playing either. Instead, try to remember that we are all different, we're all driven by different desires and goals, and we all learn things in different ways. One of the key goals for every musician is surely to feel somewhat secure in their own ability and to not feel the need to compare themselves with anyone; if you can achieve this, you'll end up happier, more fulfilled and you'll probably make better music.

Try to remain inspired by people you admire. Remember what *your* own goals are, what *you* want to achieve, work at *your* pace and see anything else as a momentary distraction. As clichéd as it may sound, no one is as good at being you as you are.

The difference between 'playing' and 'practising'

One of the fundamental issues that musician's face when deciding that they need to practise is that they don't know *how* to. Many of us will instead just 'play' because it's really fun. There is a huge difference between these two concepts, and despite most people thinking that they are the same, you'll need to be aware of the differences if you want to achieve results.

The first key difference is that practising is really hard, and so it should be. So often I will enter into conversation with a student about what they did in the week between lessons, and after some prompting, I discover that they just simply played the tune that we're learning maybe five to ten times. Despite dedicating a significant amount of time to their practising, they haven't worked on any specific aspects, and as a result, they haven't been able to make any real, tangible progress.

Playing an instrument is enjoyable and it feels really good too. You enjoy how the music flows, the tangible sensation of how your fingers feel on the strings or piano keys, you feel that you're really achieving something. Whereas practising is often dull, hard and requires a significant level of focus. Practising a piece properly (or effectively) means that you need to isolate a very small section of the music and dedicate your attention to it. Given the choice, most people will just choose to play music in the hope that they will eventually improve if they ignore the difficult bits. I'm as guilty as anyone of this, but I'm sure we can all relate to this attitude and appreciate that there is a huge difference between choosing to 'play' and deciding to 'practise'.

Why practice and experience aren't the same thing: the 10,000-hour rule

While it's easy to be seduced by the idea of being considered a master on your instrument, unsurprisingly, it's no picnic.

The 10,000-hour rule was coined by author Malcom Gladwell in his book *Outliers: The Story of Success.* In summary, Mr Gladwell concluded that 10,000 hours of deliberate practice is required by any individual in order for them to achieve a world-class level of expertise in any skill.

Can we be sure that if we practise for 10,000 hours we will achieve absolute instrumental mastery, unrivalled levels of success, followed shortly by happiness, wealth and fulfilment? No. Is this a realistic and achievable goal for absolutely everybody? Not at all, most people don't have the time to make such a commitment to their playing.

Mr Gladwell's book is well worth a read on its own merits, and while the application of this 10,000-hour rule may need to be taken with a pinch of salt, it's useful to have as a tool for explaining why practice and experience are two very different things. If we use Mr Gladwell's example and assume that 10,000 hours of practice is needed to achieve a world-class level of skill, most people working a forty hour week will bank around 1,800 hours of experience throughout the course of a year. Repeat this over six years and most workers would be close to clocking up 10,000 hours of experience in their given profession.

However, does this mean that anyone who has worked full-time for six years will have achieved a world-class level of skill in their chosen profession? Sadly not, unless they have been continually practising and pushing their ability throughout the course of their career. Since passing my driving test in 2004, I've driven a lot of miles. I'm probably not far off having spent 10,000 hours in a car but I definitely wouldn't say that my sixteen years of experience have turned me into a man with world-class skills behind the wheel – you could even argue that a few of the bad habits I've picked up have made me a less proficient driver. This is because I have accumulated lots of hours of *experience* driving a car, not a lot of hours applying deliberate and focused *practice*. The key point is not that you should worry or even think about how many hours of practice you might have accumulated, but you should instead realise that because you've been doing something the same way for a long time, achieving the same results, it doesn't mean that you're going to become an expert.

If you feel that you aren't getting the results that you want, it may be time to see if you're able to make your practice a little more effective.

PART 2: PRACTISING EFFECTIVELY IS FOR EVERYBODY

What is effective practice?

If you take one idea away from reading this book, it's that you should learn how to make all your practice as effective as possible. Effective practice is a term used to describe a specific approach to working on a skill. This method has otherwise been referred to as 'deep practice' or 'deliberate practice'. However, the core concepts are broadly the same. In fact, you can call it whatever you'd like; it's an approach that has been tested, quantified and proven to work for those who want to get serious about improving their ability.

Mr Anders Ericsson is a professor of psychology and has published a great deal of research into the psychological nature of expertise and human performance. He has been widely credited as the person whose academic research first highlighted the benefits of practising in this way. One of the key areas of his research involves testing and evaluating the impact of practising and training in the right way, a method which he refers to as 'deliberate practice'.

A lot of his research and findings on the power of practice have been discussed in great detail in the two books that I mentioned earlier: *Bounce* by Matthew Syed and *The Talent Code* by Daniel Coyle. Both of these books helped me a great deal in my own journey of compiling and creating the material for this book, and they are both what I would consider as essential reading for anyone with even a passing interest in the mechanics of peak performance.

Mr Ericsson's early 1990's study into the impact of deliberate practice involved violinists from the Music Academy of Berlin. This fascinating study may be of particular interest to musicians who are keen to better understand the key aspects of expert performance and how they work in the context of practising an instrument.

The core concepts of practising effectively

Practising effectively starts with the creation of a very specific goal, something which pushes you away from your comfort zone but which is easy to define and measure. You should aim to rehearse the skill until it becomes automatic, something you can do without thinking about it. Think about your own practice routine, provided you have one, and consider: have you ever tried to set goals in this way, or more importantly, have you really tried to push yourself out of your comfort zone?

Let's break down this approach described by Mr Ericsson into a little more detail:

1. Define a clear goal.

The goal needs to be something that you can't yet achieve, something that will take you out of your comfort zone and is on the edge of your current ability.

2. Structure and focus your practice around achieving that goal.

The nature of this practice needs to be very focussed and could be something that you plan with the help of a teacher.

3. Obtain constructive feedback and learn how to use it.

This feedback could be achieved either by recording the music that you're making yourself or perhaps using the guidance of an experienced teacher. It's crucial to understand the feedback, why you're receiving it and what you need to learn from it.

4. Integrate the skill until it becomes automatic.

The final step, and ultimately the goal, is to embed this skill into your everyday playing until it becomes automatic, allowing you to move on to your next challenge. Let's take a look at how we might apply these steps in both a practical and musical way.

Applying effective practice techniques

Our imaginary lesson begins with the teacher listening to a guitar student perform a tune that they're working on. The teacher stops the student's playing to identify a particular section of the tune that lacks clarity and fluency.

> **Teacher**: Okay, so around the start of this bar, you're not hitting the notes cleanly and the whole tune is losing fluency as a result. Could you play this four-bar section a couple of times?

The student dutifully plays the section in question.

> **Teacher**: Can *you* identify exactly where the issue is?

> **Student**: I think it's around the second half of the bar?

> **Teacher**: Almost, it's actually the three triplets which fall on beat four. They're uneven, and because they are not being played cleanly enough, the phrase loses fluency.

The teacher asks the student to play the phrase as slowly as possible so they can both focus on the movement of both hands. Together they identify a more efficient way of picking the notes of the triplet and the student takes time to adapt their technique to accommodate this change.

This is now *how* the student has to practise. In doing so, they will be practising in an effective way.

In the example above, notice how all of the steps were followed and that the advice was very specific. Also notice the way in which the teacher provided feedback; this encouraged the student to attempt to identify the necessary feedback themselves. A key aspect of teaching students at any level is to encourage them to become as self-sufficient as possible; aim to equip them with skills that they'll need to self-evaluate their own performance so they can improve their practice without even being aware they're doing it.

Practising effectively or deliberately is just an approach. It's not the only way of working towards your musical goals and there are of course other ways to approach practising. In the same way that you might decide to look at a problem from more than one perspective, could you decide to change your fundamental approach to practising, and what could that look like?

I've certainly found that some students tend to engage more with an opportunity to approach things in a creative way. This sort of approach won't necessarily be as focussed as the effective practice techniques I discussed, but it may encourage you to think differently about how you construct tasks for either yourself or your students.

Let's go back to the teacher/student dialogue. Essentially, the student is having difficulty with a very specific section of the tune they're playing. Here are some ideas which elaborate on *how* the teacher could reframe their practice routine to enable the learning process to become creative and interesting:

- Change the notes at the start of the bar and give the student a new perspective as they play into the difficult phrase.
- Change the notes after the difficult phrase.
- Change the key and reposition the phrase on the instrument so that it can be played with open strings.
- Sing the notes of the phrase, ascending and descending.
- Ask them to record themselves playing the phrase, watch it back and write a critical evaluation of their own playing.

- Write a short melody which uses all the notes from the bar, in the same order, but change all of the rhythms.

Some of these points will seem arbitrary through the eyes of a lot of people, and these are definitely not ideas that would work for every student. However, sometimes those little breakthroughs come from thinking in a way that's different from the norm and one which takes you away from your comfort zone.

The science bit: that magic myelin stuff

In order to better understand the principles of practising effectively and the importance of repetition in acquiring skill, it's worth delving a little deeper into what actually happens to our brains when learning a skill. Let's take a brief look at something called myelin.

Myelin is an insulating layer of fatty protein that wraps around our nerve fibres. Through careful and deliberate repetition of a skill, we insulate our nerves with more of this protein, gradually increasing the speed and efficiency at which we can perform that skill. Myelin works as insulation for our nerve fibres, and it builds up over time as we repeatedly fire impulses to the brain. The more we repeat the skill through practice, the more the myelin does its job, allowing us to perform the skill more efficiently, eventually until it becomes automatic.

The numerous studies proving how myelin is acquired and why it's so essential in building expertise illustrate that there is scientific evidence demonstrating how essential the repetition of skill is in the practice process. We don't need to fall back on the lazy assumption that the majority of someone's 'talent' or natural skill is given to them at birth; scientific evidence shows us how anyone can get better at anything with the right practice process in place.

For a deeper understanding of the role of myelin in building skill, I would again highly recommend Daniel Coyle's book, *The Talent Code*.

The importance of goal setting

While it's essential to ensure that you are practising in a way which is as effective as possible, setting small, achievable goals is a big part of that process. When I was studying music, I never really thought about goal setting because I was just playing lots of music and it never occurred to me that setting goals would really help.

Having some sort of tangible goal or target to aim for undeniably focusses the mind in a way which is hard to achieve otherwise. Knowing that you've got a music exam fast approaching or that you've got to be able to manage to complete that five-kilometre park run in a couple of weeks' time will undoubtedly scare you into practice and/or training.

However, as a musician, it's sometimes harder to set tangible goals when your only real motivation is to make music. It's easier for a sportsperson to set goals related to levels of fitness or strength, but arguably, those pursuing success in creative industries have a harder time defining exactly what they want to achieve and, more importantly, how they're going to get there.

It's important to understand the difference between definable goals and non-definable goals. An example of a clearly definable goal could be:

- Be able to play from memory all five positions of the F major scale on the guitar.

This is easy to quantify. You can either do it or you can't, it's pretty binary. You keep practising until you can do it, and when you can, it's fairly easy to admit to yourself that you've got it right – job done.

An example of a non-definable goal would instead be:

- Be able to fluently improvise a solo over a chord progression in the key of F major, while demonstrating a vast array of highly technical skill and harmonic sophistication, similar to that guy I saw on YouTube.

This is not a definable goal. It's very hard to work towards because it will mean vastly different things to different people. A non-definable goal needs to be broken down into smaller chunks so that you're able to practise effectively. This goal above could be broken into a number of progressive stages which could act as a map, all pointing you somewhat closer to achieving your initial, broader objective.

As an example, we could attempt to decode the statement above and split it into some more easily definable objectives. How about:

- Learn to play the F major scale horizontally across the fretboard on every string.
- Learn to play the F major scale ascending and descending in intervals of thirds, fourths, fifths, sixths and sevenths.
- Transcribe and learn to play the solo of that guy on YouTube.
- Transcribe three of your favourite solos in F major and incorporate parts of these solos into your own playing.
- Learn to sing the F major scale.

You could seemingly go on forever, listing exercises and ideas which loosely relate to our original idea, but because music is such a subjective process, you must set goals which are largely objective.

The key point here is that goal setting is really important. Whether you're a student or teacher, if you want to practise effectively, you need to set goals for yourself or your students which are easily definable. This doesn't mean that you can't be creative, nor does it mean that you have to be constantly measuring every little bit of progress you make. Be aware of how goal setting can improve your playing, but more importantly, what a difference it can make to your own mental well-being. Knowing that you've created, worked towards and attained your own target is a hugely satisfying achievement.

Occasionally try to give yourself a target which has to be completed within a week or so; it's a brilliant way of focussing your mind. It could just be something relatively straightforward like learning four bars of a B. B. King solo. The aim is to achieve focus through being clear about what it is you want and providing yourself with a timeline for achieving it.

Shortcuts?

There aren't any.

Be sure to repeat this to yourself and/or any of your students who may be serious about studying music.

If the internet tells you that you can become a guitar hero in under an hour with minimal effort, you are being lied to. If someone else tells you that they went from being a complete beginner to a professional musician only using a thirty-minute online course and they did this by only practising for two hours a week then they are delusional.

You need to prepare for the fact that worthwhile results require worthwhile levels of commitment. In the interests of managing your own expectations, recognise that you should always set yourself audacious goals, and that by doing this, you must appreciate that you'll need to go above and beyond in terms of effort and commitment and be prepared to take a long-term view.

With that in mind, we now move on from effective practice to instead consider some of the deeper psychological factors that have a huge impact on our ability to practise and learn music.

PART 3: THE TOOLS

This is the part of the book where we really start to look at a bigger picture. We're a long way from 'No, that's actually a G sharp' or 'Make sure you practise your scales this week.' Instead, things become a little more abstract. In all my years of teaching and learning, I've tried to understand the deeper issues that have affected my own progress and that of my students. I've broken these down into six aspects, which if you're able to become aware of, I can guarantee will change the way you think about the learning process.

You might decide to call these something dramatic such as the 'Pillars of practice', 'The essentials of improvement' or 'Six things which guarantee to bring you unlimited wealth and success', but it's probably better that you ignore those altogether.

Instead, take a read through and think about how you perceive each of these elements; are they important to you? If you thought about one of them differently, could it make a difference to your music?

Okay, so brace yourself, this is usually the sort of

catchphrase that you'd find in a LinkedIn post, adorned with photos of sunsets in the background, but I can't think of a better way of summarising the next part of the book:

> By finding **Inspiration** in music, we discover the **Motivation** to practise. We then ignore **Distractions** in order to be able to **Focus** on what we want. From this, we constantly learn from our **Failures** to eventually achieve **Success**.

Inspiration

Inspiration is where it all starts. There was hopefully something or someone who inspired you to pick up an instrument in the first place, or at least persuade you to take it all a bit more seriously. You can find inspiration in the strangest of places, and it's important to ensure that you're on the lookout for it all the time.

Okay, so you could file inspiration under the same heading as motivation, a lot of people would suggest they are the same thing. While they're similar, motivation is something that drives you from an outside or external source; you may be motivated to practise for your Grade 6 music exam because if you get enough UCAS points, you're more likely to get that place at university. Whereas, you may have been inspired to write music all afternoon because you heard a particularly great song and this reaffirmed your desire to write and create music which resonates with you.

Inspiration is a driving force from inside yourself, it's something a little deeper than motivation. It's harder to force inspiration, but it could come from speaking to someone, reading a book, watching a video or going for a walk; it can be found anywhere. I want this book to *inspire* people to get excited about practising music because inspiration can be an enormously powerful thing.

It's natural to feel completely uninspired about music from time to time. It's common to feel this way after something that didn't go right; perhaps it was a bad gig, audition or a frustrating lesson. This feeling can also occur following a period where you've actually been playing a lot of music but things have started to just feel stale and repetitive. This discourages you from practising and the guilt starts to set in, adding momentum to the cycle – only making you feel worse.

Rather than overanalysing why you feel like this, perhaps you should just put the instrument down and try doing something that you haven't done for a while:

- Go to see lots of good live music.
- Put your instrument away and don't play it for a week, or longer. Did you miss it, why?
- Set time aside to *really* listen to music, no distractions, no phone, no internet.
- Think about why you picked up the instrument in the first place.
- Take your instrument apart completely, clean it properly and leave it in the corner of the room until you feel like playing again.
- Go for a long walk.

Look at things differently, try to learn something that you would have never otherwise considered. The feeling that you lack inspiration is often a sign that you need a break from what you have been doing and you need a new challenge. If you've been using a strict practice schedule, get rid of it.

Take time to remind yourself of the reasons that you started learning music in the first place.

Motivation

It's fairly difficult to motivate yourself to do anything unless you have some sort of genuine incentive to do so. All of our decisions are guided by incentives which drive us to work towards our financial, moral, musical and aspirational goals. What is it that motivates you to practise? Are you keen to impress others? Or are you just thinking of all the lovely cash that you're bound to make once you learn all of your scales? In a lot of cases, having the 'right' kind of motivation can be the key to determining how likely you are to achieve what you want.

So, how do we determine what is the 'right' kind of motivation?

I personally think that if your sole motivation for doing something is derived from external factors such as financial success or wishing to impress others, then it's a dangerous route to take. While there is absolutely nothing wrong with being financially motivated, it should be considered to be a by-product of your eventual success. In my opinion, the best results are achieved by being motivated by internal factors or things you are in control of. So, this could mean that your sole motivation to practise is just simply wanting to become a better musician because you are driven to become better at playing music, setting you on the path to eventually becoming a better teacher and performer.

When devising your practice goals, start by considering what might actually be motivating you. Ask yourself the question: 'Is that going to be enough to make me want to get out of bed at 5 a.m. to pick up my instrument?' Real motivation could drive you to cultivate an almost obsessive attitude towards practice and progress, while doing it all for the 'right' reasons. This doesn't mean that you need to go without a social life, but a little healthy obsession could be a good thing.

Right reasons?

Simply knowing that you *should* be practising something isn't enough of a motivation to do so. In order to summon the necessary levels of motivation, you may need to look at things another way. Let's look at sight-reading as an example, and let's say that you want to improve your ability to play music from sight. Sight-reading is often the most dreaded activity of all musicians, and it's fair to assume that the vast majority of even experienced professional musicians would identify it as one of their weaknesses.

Instead of feeling that you should be studying the little black dots regularly because your teacher keeps telling you how great they are, try to look at it in another way:

> Have you considered what a huge impact reading from sight may have on your ability to understand the language of music in general?

It's fair to say that your understanding of how advanced rhythms work will improve with some sight-reading focus.

How about your employability as a musician? There is always a demand for players who can 'read'.

Your ability to sight-read could set you apart from other musicians competing for the same gig or audition. Did I mention that it would undoubtedly improve your ability to read and write music?

Have you heard the *Strictly Come Dancing* band off the telly? All the people in that band can read music pretty well. That could be something cool to aim for, right?

How about the impact it could have on developing your musical ear?

One of the brilliant things about music is that, in the end, it's all related. If you can convince yourself of the fact that there is always more than one reason for working on something, then there is always going to be more than one thing that you'll be able to gain from doing so.

Distraction

It's best to just accept that you will become distracted from time to time; it's an absolute inevitability whilst practising music. I find that distractions are hardest to ignore when I'm trying to make a start to something; I've experienced no end of distractions while writing this book for instance. A lot of hours spent trying to write and plan weren't particularly productive, but I often found that if you can get through the first ten minutes or so then you'll really start to gain some momentum, and the distractions suddenly aren't so distracting.

Sometimes distractions can just be a sign that your brain needs to take a break, and it's important not to feel bad about this. It's easy to be convinced of ludicrous mantras about how you should only sleep for two hours a night and work or practise every other hour or you're destined for failure. Taking a break is okay; in fact, it's essential if you wish to avoid distractions. The key message of this book is not necessarily about practising harder for longer, but instead making the best of the time that you do have; being aware of distractions and knowing how to deal with them is also essential.

I use some very basic steps to help me avoid distractions and ensure that I get the most out of any time I'm able to commit to music. Some of these may seem obvious, but have you ever actually tried to apply any of the following?

- Treat your practice time as if it were a pre-arranged meeting. You can't get out of it, that thirty minutes after lunch is going to be you, sitting with an instrument and that's it.
- Turn off the Wi-Fi on your phone and laptop during your practice sessions.
- Know exactly what you're going to work on during the practice session.
- Don't watch the clock unless you need to. If you can spend a little longer, why wouldn't you?
- Remind yourself of why you've set yourself your goals and think about what it is that you're working towards.
- If you're constantly distracted, maybe you aren't motivated enough – is it time to reassess what's motivating you?

It's amazing how quickly you'll be able to form habits. If you can introduce a few of the changes above or create a few of your own, you'll be able to reduce the distractions that arise, ensuring that you get more from your practice time.

Focus

I suppose that distraction and focus can be found at opposite ends of the spectrum; you need to get rid of one in order to be able to find the other. However, I want to talk more specifically about why it's important to focus on one area of your music at a time; why I believe that meticulously dividing up your time across many areas of study stops you from achieving any real focus.

You need to work on your tone, your timing needs work, you could also do with expanding your repertoire, or how about that daily sight-reading practice that you committed to last week? It's easy to become overwhelmed with the amount of stuff you feel you should be doing as someone who is serious about studying music. Unless you're a relative beginner or are fairly new to learning music, I don't believe that having a long list of things that you're attempting to work on all at once is a good idea.

Below, I've shown an example of the sort of practice schedule that I would draw up for myself when I started to get serious about studying music. I was keen to excel in as many areas as possible and

I was convinced that I needed to do a bit of everything, every day:

Warm Up

Technique:

Alternate picking – 30 minutes

Left-hand legato – 30 minutes

Pentatonic Drills – 30 minutes

Theory:

Sight-Reading – 30 minutes

Scale shapes (circle of fifths) – 30 minutes

Improvisation – 30 minutes

Aural:

Ear Training – 20 minutes

Interval recognition – 15 minutes

Besides the fact that I would rarely ever stick with any of these schedules for much longer than a few days, the overall quality of the practice was poor because I didn't dwell on any one specific area for long enough to achieve focus. Have you ever found that with some tasks, even those you are keen to begin, the first ten or so minutes can often feel quite slow as you mentally adjust to making a start? I've always noticed this reluctance present in both myself and many of my students, but once you've been able to pass through the first five to ten minutes, you begin to feel momentum building and distractions slowly seem to disappear, right? It took me years to discover that there was a better way of achieving focus, and I've since found that the very best results are achieved by focussing on just one thing until you can do it.

There are of course instances where you may have to divide up your practice time into a few different areas. For instance, if you're a complete beginner you will probably find that you need to maintain some sort of variety within your practice time in order to remain interested and motivated. However, as you become a more proficient musician and wish to progress further, sooner or later you need to recognise that adopting focus and not spreading your time too sparsely is the only way to make progress.

Here are a few ideas to help you think about how you could change your focus:

- Be creative with the way that you practise. For example, could you find ways to combine working on your repertoire and technical skills at the same time?
- Set yourself short achievable goals; what could you achieve in a week if *all* of your practice for that week was dedicated to just sight-reading, just repertoire, or just writing music?
- Find a way of giving yourself a deadline: book a recording date, schedule an exam, or learn something for a particular gig or performance.
- Throw your old practice schedule away (if you had one). See what happens when you change your whole approach.
- Take a break from music for a couple of days and don't feel bad about it.
- Mow the lawn.

Usually, if you're trying to deal with an obstacle and your approach isn't working, reassessing how you're actually approaching the problem is the only logical solution. If you struggle to focus during your practice time, turn things on their head and narrow your area of focus. I used to worry that if I didn't keep on top of my technique then my playing would become sloppy, or, if I went a few days without practising scales, then I'd forget them all. The reality is, our brains are pretty incredible. A few days away from a rigid schedule could provide an opportunity to concentrate your efforts towards achieving a series of small, manageable goals which focus on one area of your music. Setting targets which are fairly easily attainable in a short space of time can also provide you with a temporary psychological boost, allowing you to feel good about music, motivating you to practise more, set more goals – we could be on to something here.

Failure

Understanding the importance of failure and the role it plays is the most valuable tool in your quest for continued musical improvement. If you try to shield yourself entirely from any sort of failure, then you are unlikely to want to try anything new. It's also fairly likely to assume that unless you are able to gradually build up resilience, then you won't really ever succeed at anything.

Failure is a pretty harsh word, and the immediate connotations of failing elicit a negative reaction; perhaps you're just not good enough or you just haven't got the skill required. These instant reactions encourage a binary approach to the problem, either winning or losing. Failure (or not succeeding straight away) is an inevitable part of the process when learning anything. The next step is deciding how to deal with it; finding out what didn't go right, why this was the case and what you need to work on to improve.

Feeling like you've failed on a performance

Let's discuss failure in the context of a musical performance. It could perhaps be a music exam, concert, playing with friends or a live gig that left you feeling down and disappointed. In most cases a performance can be one of the most nerve-wracking of experiences. Your musical skill is open to the scrutiny of others and it's something which you'll probably reflect on for years to come; it's impossible not to feel the pressure. Maybe nerves got the better of you; it didn't sound good, did you forget the chords, the melody? All of these thoughts and concerns are inevitable.

During a performance you can suddenly become very aware of your own existence, and as a result, the performance of music immediately takes a back seat. A performance which you felt didn't go right can be very hard to deal with, particularly when you feel that you could've done so much better. You start to question why you bother playing an instrument when the reality of performing is so detached from the enjoyment that you experience from playing at home or in lessons.

However, the silver lining is to be found in how you react to it and what you do with it; take some comfort in the fact that everybody has failed. The Beatles were rejected by Decca Records, Elvis Presley was told that he couldn't sing and Walt Disney was told that he 'lacked imagination'.

That's great, but what can you do about it?

A 'bad' performance will mean a number of different things to different people. However, it's actually a wonderful thing.

Your perceived failure will have highlighted the areas in which you are least comfortable. No matter how disastrously you may have felt the performance went, it's unlikely it was as absolutely catastrophic as it made you feel at the time. The reason things may not have gone quite as planned was not necessarily because you hadn't practised enough or that you weren't concentrating but more likely because while you've spent a lot of hours playing and practising music, you haven't spent nearly as many gaining the necessary experience in performing.

Performing live presents a very different dynamic from that of life in the practice room. Professional bands and performers will have had hundreds, potentially thousands of hours of individual experience on stage which has enabled them to reach a point where they feel relaxed and able to deliver a great performance.

Don't beat yourself up about it. No one expects your performance to be perfect every time. Try to take a completely different perspective on the whole thing. How about you just admit that your first live performance won't be perfect and resign yourself to the fact that you'll probably feel some nerves for a while when playing in front of others. It may even take you years to feel comfortable on stage. It may even take a hundred performances before you feel like you've played your best while performing live. This may actually start to make you feel better, take the pressure off – take the view that some form of failure at first is absolutely inevitable; don't fear it, embrace it.

Bad performances had a major effect on me when I started getting serious about music, for which I blamed myself entirely. In fact, it nearly put me off playing music altogether, but after a while, once I understood that the odd bad performance was really just an inevitable part of the process, things weren't so bad, and I discovered a way of using feedback to learn, become more resilient and make my practice more effective.

If you've had moments where you've felt as if things haven't gone right, think about how you might answer some of these questions:

- Starting with the least successful, list the aspects of the performance which didn't go well.
- Reflect on what did actually go well. It's likely that the good parts outweighed the bad.
- How do you think that other people perceived it? How good/bad do you think they thought you played?
- What scared you most about the whole thing?
- What are the actual repercussions? What's now the worse than can happen?
- How is this performance going to change how you practise?

Using failure constructively

The reason that I go on about failure so much and keep saying how great it is, is because it's the most valuable form of feedback that we are likely to receive. It enables us to understand, in significant detail, the aspects of music that we need to improve on, whether this feedback tells us that we just need to obtain more experience playing live or provides us with something more nuanced, maybe that we need to really work on our sense of musical timing when playing sixteenth notes at 128bpm.

One of the core concepts of practising effectively, discussed earlier in the book, was to 'obtain constructive feedback and learn how to use it'. This is all that you're doing when you feel as if you're failing – using the feedback gathered from negative experiences to enable yourself to make better music. Try to remember this the next time you feel that something didn't go right; it's just part of the process, so don't worry about it.

Success

I believe that it's essential to seize every suitable opportunity you can to celebrate your successes in life and music, no matter how small they may seem. In order to justify any amount of time that you've dedicated to music, it's crucial to feel that you have been able to achieve something and remember that it's important to feel good about it.

It's very difficult not to compare your success to that of everyone else, often making you feel as if your version of success actually wasn't that great.

It's very important to remember that all success is relative.

If you are constantly comparing yourself to everyone else, no matter how much you achieve, you will never really feel successful. There will always be someone else who you *perceive* to be bigger, louder, richer or cooler, or another musician who has more online followers, a better website, more musical skill, or more weekly students. But as soon as you're able to appreciate that *your* success is relative to *your* goals and direction then it can feel quite liberating. You don't need to worry about what anyone else is doing and you can focus on exactly what you want. This all eventually leads to the rather deep and somewhat profound question that we should all ask ourselves:

What do I have to do to consider myself to be successful?

Notice that you're not asking 'What do I need to do to be considered successful by others', but instead 'What does success actually mean to me?'

Starting with what you actually want to achieve brings us back to the core concepts of effective practice. However, in this instance we're thinking about what we want in broader terms. Instead of working towards nailing your harmonic minor scales across three octaves, what do you want to achieve with music? Responses to this question will of course vary greatly depending on whether you see music as a career or not. If you're planning on a career in music, or indeed already have one, think about the goals you want to achieve over the very long term as this can help to inform what you need to get done over the next couple of months.

What do I want and how do I get it?

For instance, let's say that your five-year plan is to leave your job and just be able to play, record and teach music full-time – you can really start to break down where you need to be in the next year or two. You may conclude that within the next year you need to have completed that teaching qualification and have acquired ten weekly students. That's great, now what do you need to do within the next week to ensure that you keep on track?

Personally, I'm all for planning, but scheduling every week of your life isn't for everyone. My point is that even the most seemingly ambitious goals are completely achievable if you're willing to break them down into more digestible chunks and remain focussed.

When I started out studying music, my end goal was eventually to be able to make a living through teaching and playing guitar. This end goal was preceded by the completion of a lot of smaller, easily attainable goals over the coming years. When I eventually got there, it felt good, but it's easy to take it all for granted, and it's hard not to feel as if you need to immediately focus on the next thing: more, bigger, better.

Success to you may just mean being good enough to play in a band, recording your first album or something bigger like landing a big gig with an orchestra or touring band. Success is the culmination of all your hard work, the last step and the one which needs to be savoured and enjoyed. If you are ever starting to feel despondent about your successes, it may just be a case of ensuring that you manage your own expectations about what can be achieved. So often, those who start off learning to play an instrument convince themselves that they will be able to dedicate countless hours of the week to practising, promising themselves that they will be able to achieve amazing things in a remarkably short space of time. That's not to say that you should not set yourself audacious goals in every area of your life, because you should. However, if you work sixty hours a week and have a busy family life, you may struggle to practise for three hours every day – it may just be a case of setting short obtainable goals to keep you motivated over the long term, ensuring you feel what it's like to achieve your version of success.

Don't ever feel guilty about taking a day off; remember how far you've come. Music is such that you will never stop learning, and this should serve as a motivation for you to develop a tireless attitude towards becoming better and always feeling good about it.

The problem with books like this one

Up until now, we've assumed that if you set yourself goals, applying the concepts of deliberate practice, while considering how stuff like motivation and failure can impact your progress, then you will get to where you want to be. Problem solved, eternal happiness achieved, and bank balance restored. But of course, it isn't always as simple as that. What if we conclude that we are in fact being *too* specific? For example, your issue is that you're stuck in a rut and you feel as if your improvising sounds stale, repetitive and you're not generating any new ideas. So, you drill down and really think about what it is that you're struggling with, but this doesn't generate any specific answers either. You conclude that you know enough scale shapes, can apply enough musical phrases, you understand how chord progressions work, but still you're not able to create any new solutions. Let's take this all apart and perhaps use some creativity to figure out what you could do to help yourself.

Keep it simple

A common issue is that, without realising it, students try to run before they can walk. They try to attempt to apply and understand complicated concepts before they have absolutely mastered the basics. It's no use trying to understand advanced chord substitutions if you can't play a major scale, right? You must be really honest with yourself about how well you *actually* know something. It's often useful to seek a second opinion: consult a good teacher, book a few lessons and see whether it's worth going back to basics for a short time. There isn't any shame in starting again with a few basic scale shapes. It's very important to remember that the very best musicians are brilliant at playing the simplest things with absolute accuracy and making them sound great, every time.

Let's assume that you have concluded that your skills as an improvisor are limited; it seems as if you are stuck in a rut and feel confined to a few of the same scale shapes and ideas. Your biggest issue is that there isn't a specific problem, therefore there isn't a specific solution. Often, in this case, the best approach is to start by applying some simple approaches but be sure to establish goals and outcomes which are easy to define – remember those from earlier?

Practice Approach One: Go back to basics with your scale knowledge.

Construct a practice routine based on learning all the relevant scales. Create a list of the scales then divide them into groups based on tonality. Then, learn them in all possible positions/octaves on your instrument, playing them along with a metronome. If you make a mistake – start again. Don't assume that you already know them just because you perceive them to be simple; in my opinion, you can't really ever learn something well enough.

Practice Approach Two: Learn to internalise the music.

I'm always trying to convince my students to sing scales and musical phrases. I've found it to be a pretty amazing way of transforming your musical ear. Construct a practice routine based on singing the major and minor scales in as many octaves as possible. Then create your own short musical phrases by singing them, without using your instrument.

Practice Approach Three: Learn from your heroes.

Pick three instrumental solos from any of your favourite artists/musicians and learn to play them.

Ideally, at least one of them should be one which was played on an instrument different from yours. Copy the phrasing, timing and tone as close as you can and play along to the recording.

Because there wasn't a specific problem, you have to try a few different approaches. The ideas above are based on the fact that if nothing else is working you maybe need to go back to basics. So many students think they know all of the scales well enough, and they often don't. So many students are unable to sing a major scale, which is one of the fundamental blocks on which we build music. One of the marvels of music is that you never stop learning, and it's a positive thing to realise that no one can ever really say, 'Okay, I'm done.' Try to be as creative about how you approach practising as you are when you create music.

PART 4: THE PRACTICE PLAN

I've always attempted to use practice plans both for myself and for use in my lessons, but I never managed to stick with them. However, throughout my years of teaching, I've experimented with a load of different ideas with regards to how I'd like a template for practice to look, based on how students tend to respond to targets and goals. I don't believe that practice should be focussed on many different areas all at once but should instead be directed towards one core aim, accompanied by a clear plan of how to achieve it.

Not everyone is going to want to use practice plans. This is simply because everybody learns in a different way and having to follow rigid rules can be a tedious process for a lot of people. Nonetheless, you may find that the plan encourages you to think differently or prompt you to try them out if you have students of your own.

The plan that follows is somewhat malleable. You can sculpt it, adapt it or you can just completely ignore it altogether. However, the questions encourage you to apply a lot of the approaches discussed in this book: specificity, goal setting, acknowledging failure and understanding your own motivation for doing something. In order for these to work, you need to be honest with yourself and follow the questions reasonably closely.

To give you a practical idea of how these plans can be used, I've filled out an example which outlines how you might use it to work towards a goal, along with a clear description of the information you'd need to include. Notice how specific everything is. There is little room for ambiguity!

The blank practice plan and example plan are available to download free from my website here:

learnguitarwithcharlie.com/the-practice-plan

So go ahead and enjoy, apply and peruse the following. I don't believe in timing your practice sessions, it's up to you how long you spend on a given area of music. Be as honest with yourself as you can and remember how important it is to ensure that your goals are specific and measurable.

The Practice Template

What do you want to achieve?

Be as specific as you can and provide as much detail as possible. The more specific your goal, the easier it will be to work towards and achieve.

Example:
Memorise and perform all major and natural minor scale shapes in every key, over two octaves in any position on the guitar.

How are you going to do this?

Break down your practice process into at least three actions that you are going to take in order to achieve what you want – use as many additional actions as you like. These actions don't need to be in any specific order.

Example:
1. *Apply the principles of the 'CAGED' system (exclusive to guitar players) to break down the scales into shapes which relate to open chords.*

2. *Practise, for example, G major followed by G natural minor in the same position to spot similarities and differences between the notes in each scale.*

3. *Practise every shape in each position and cycle through the keys in fourths.*

4. *Use a metronome to gauge your progress and consistency.*

5. *Cycle through all twelve keys, playing each scale without changing position and without making any mistakes. Then progress onto the next fretboard position.*

Are you going to give yourself a timeframe to achieve your goal? If so, how long?

It's often better to work towards shorter, more achievable goals. Aim to create goals that you think you can realistically achieve within an absolute maximum of three months.

Example:
Six weeks. I already have a reasonable command of these scale shapes, but I realise that I need to really study them for them to feel automatic.

How are you going to measure your success?

This is dependent on how much thought you have given to your initial goal. It's essential that you find a way of measuring your success. You must be able to define what your desired outcome is here.

Example:
The scales need to be played as quavers at 80bpm, fluently and without any mistakes. A four-beat rest is allowed each time I change key.

What is your motivation for working towards this goal, and when you lack motivation, how are you going to find it?

Be honest about why you actually want to do this. This can sometimes be very difficult but it all comes back to what you want the outcomes to be. Also suggest some ways in which you might be able to find inspiration or motivation again if needed. These could be unrelated to playing an instrument.

Example:
I want to achieve a better understanding of the fretboard as I've identified gaps in my knowledge of scales. I also know that a strong knowledge of major and minor scales will help me to apply modal scales, in addition to providing me with more options to use across the neck when improvising.

I really enjoy watching Jaco Pastorius' Modern Electric Bass videos. His command of the instrument is utterly inspiring, and I use his videos as a way of inspiring me to work towards achieving a greater level of fluency in my playing.

Identify the things that you think you are going to find difficult during this process.

Try to foresee any difficulties which you are likely to experience where possible. Suggest some ways in which you might be able to overcome these problems.

Example:
The lesser used keys are difficult to remember; Db, Gb, Eb and Ab are not keys that I commonly use. I will spend the majority of my practice time working on the scale shapes from these keys.

Epilogue

Shortly after I started researching and compiling the chapters for this book, I was discussing various ideas relating to practice with an old friend of mine who casually observed: 'Well, yeah – you get better at what you do a lot of, don't you?' He said it in a way that suggested it was the most obvious thing in the world, yet I suppose that it perfectly summarises, in the most concise way possible, why practice works. It's true as well, of course, that repetition of a skill is at the heart of getting better; the more you repeat something, whether it be public speaking, accountancy or writing epilogues, the more you will improve, and that, by itself, may be more than enough for most people.

Some of the books that I've most enjoyed have encouraged me to think about and understand the processes which relate to how and why something works. This really is all that I'm looking to achieve with this book, and I hope that this in turn helps people to become more fulfilled by their own musical endeavours. It's important to remain open-minded because of the ease by which we can develop tunnel vision about our own approaches, refusing to entertain the idea that something else might just work. I would urge anyone (including myself) to always consider that there is another way of approaching something, and sometimes better results can be achieved by forgetting everything and trusting a new path.

Practice can become addictive. The thrill of knowing that a small improvement in your playing is due to that specific focus that you applied to your music that week or month is an extremely rewarding feeling. This will then likely encourage you to practise more, continuing a pattern of improvement and fulfilment. Sadly, it won't always feel like this of course, and that's the reason we need to be aware of the deeper aspects of the process, understanding how and why practice works so that we can build habits, adapting our approach to suit our lifestyle and personal goals.

References:

Covey, Stephen, *The 7 Habits of Highly Effective People,* (New York: Free Press, 1989).

Coyle, Daniel, *The Talent Code: Greatness isn't born. It's grown,* (London: Random House, 2009).

Ericsson, K. Anders; Smith Jacqui, *Toward a General Theory of Expertise: Prospects and Limits,* (Cambridge: Cambridge University Press, 1991).

Gladwell, Malcolm, *Outliers: The Story of Success,* (London: Penguin, 2008).

Syed, Matthew, *Bounce: The Myth of Talent and the Power of Practice,* (London: Harper Collins, 2010).

Made in United States
Troutdale, OR
12/03/2025

42982802R00042